JOURNEY TO THE PAST

IMPERIAL ROME

Mario Denti

RAINTREE
STECK-VAUGHN
PUBLISHERS

A Harcourt Company

Austin · New York
www.steck-vaughn.com

Published by Raintree Steck-Vaughn, an imprint of Steck-Vaughn Company

Library of Congress Cataloging-in-Publication Data

Denti, Mario.
   Imperial Rome / Mario Denti.
      p. cm. — (Journey to the past)
   Includes index.
   ISBN 0-7398-1952-6
     1. Rome—Civilization—Juvenile literature. [1. Rome—Civilization.]
   I. Title.   II. Series.

DG77 .46 2001
937—dc21   00-059209

Project Director: Marco Drago, Andrea Boroli
Editorial Director: Cristina Cappa Legora
Editorial Coordinator: Cristina Drago
Translated by: Mary Stuttard

Author: Mario Denti
Illustration: Aldo Ripamonti; Carlo Stanga, Piergiorgio Citterio
Art Director: Marco Volpati
Raintree Steck-Vaughn Staff: Marion Bracken, Pam Wells
Project Manager: Lyda Guz
Photo Research: Claudette Landry, Sarah Fraser

Photo Credits:

P.48c ©CORBIS/Dave Bartruff; p.49a ©CORBIS/ Araldo de Luca; p.49b ©CORBIS/Archivo Iconagrafico, S.A.; p. 49c ©CORBIS; p.50a ©M. Mastror- illo/The Stock Market; p.50b ©CORBIS/Angelo Homal; p.50c ©CORBIS/ Michael S. Yamashita; p.51a ©CORBIS/Carmen Redondo; p.51b ©CORBIS/ Andrea Jemolo; p.51c ©CORBIS/Rugger Vanni.

All other photographs are from the Archives of IGDA.

Printed in Italy

1 2 3 4 5 6 7 8 9   04 03 02 01

TABLE OF CONTENTS

All Roads Lead to Rome

Reaching Rome from any one of the many cities or provinces in the Empire is not always easy in spite of the fact that Roman territories boast one of the most impressive road networks ever constructed. The roads, which connect even the most distant places, were designed above all to be used by the army. They had to ensure the fastest possible transfer of the legions from one place to another. They were vital to an efficient postal service, too. When you travel these roads, it is not unusual to meet couriers on horseback who are able to ride up to 100 miles a day! They change horses at *stationes* placed 8 to 12 miles apart. However to go as far as the great city of Rome, you have to overcome a series of obstacles. The first is time. The journey, especially by cart or riding a mule, is extremely slow. A traveler coming from Greece who lands at

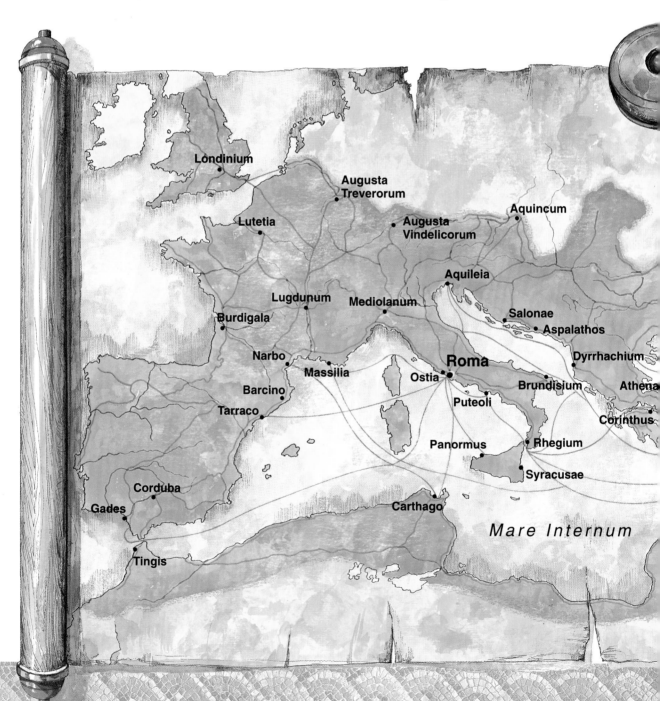

Brundisium will take another 12 days to reach Rome! This is why goods often travel by sea, along routes that are quicker and more convenient. The second obstacle is the risk of attack by bandits.

Traveling by night in some regions is extremely hazardous. You had better have an escort! Comfortable hotels are hard to find. The hotels that offer travelers lodging are no more than low-level taverns. They are filthy, foul-smelling, and used frequently by people whose intentions are questionable.

By Land and Sea

The time required to travel by land depends most of all on the season. In summer you can travel twice as fast as in winter. The days are longer, the weather better, and the roads are in good condition. You could travel 12 miles a day by cart in summer and just over half that distance in winter. On the other hand, short distances can be covered much quicker on horseback, changing your mount at two or more *stationes*, or stops, per day.

Distances by land between Rome and the principal cities in the empire (in miles):

from Lutetia to Rome	*1,000*
from Corduba to Rome	*1,200*
from Lugdunum to Rome	*800*
from Brundisium to Rome	*400*
from Massilia to Rome	*750*
from Mediolanum to Rome	*500*
from Rome to Puteoli	*133*

Time taken to sail between the major Roman ports (in number of days' sailing)

from Gades to Ostia	*9*
from Carthago to Ostia	*3/5*
from Alexandria to Puteoli	*20*
from Narbo to Ostia	*3*
from Tarraco to Ostia	*6*
from Massilia to Ostia	*3*
from Puteoli to Reghium	*2*
from Caesaria to Ostia	*20*
from Athenae to Ostia	*10*

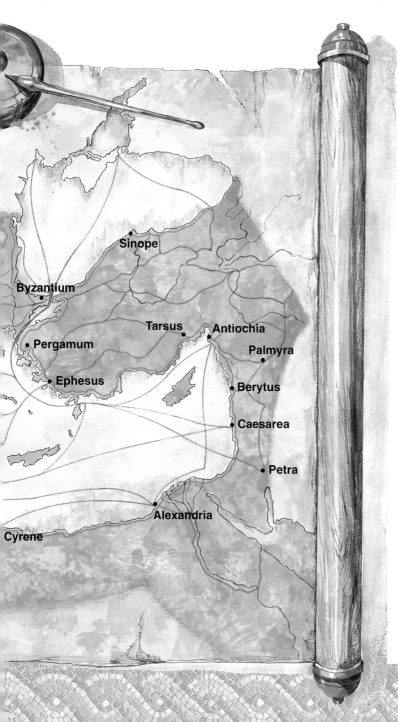

(Roman place names and their modern equivalents)
Alexandria/Alexandria (Egypt); Antiochia/ Antioch; Aquileia/ Aquileia; Aquincum/Budapest; Aspalathos/Spalatum; Athenae/Athens; Augusta Treverorum/Trier; Augusta Vindelicorum/Augsberg; Barcino/Barcellona; Berytus/Beirut; Brundisium/Brindisi; Burdigala/Bordeaux; Byzantium/ Istanbul; Carthago/Carthage; Caesarea/Cesarea; Corduba/ Cordoba; Corinthus/Corinth; Cyrene/Cyrene; Dyrrhachium/ Durazzo or Durres; Ephesus/Ephesus; Gades/Cadiz; Londinium/London; Lugdunum/Lyons; Lutetia/Paris; Mare Internum/Mediterranean Sea; Marssilia/Marseilles; Mediolanum/Milan; Narbo/Narbonne; Ostia/Ostia; Palmyra/Palmyra or Tadmur; Panormus/Palermo; Pergamum/ Pergamum or Bergama; Petra/Petra; Puteoli/Pozzuolo; Rhegium/Reggio Calabria; Salonae/Salonae or Solin; Sinope/Sinop; Syracusae/Syracuse; Tarraco/Tarragona; Tarsus/Tarsus; Tingis/Tangiers.

Welcome!

So here we are at the gates of Rome! Once through the outer city walls, built only recently by the Emperor Aurelian, you find another ring of much older city walls, called the Servian walls (named after Servius Tullius, the sixth king of Rome). Parked near the gates you can see the Roman version of a taxicab. Special coaches, or *cisiarii*, a real form of public transportation, are ready to whisk you rapidly to the heart of the city. Carts carrying goods or supplies have to wait

until nightfall to enter the walls. They are banned by law from crossing the built-up part of the capital during daylight hours. But this does not mean that the streets are calm and quiet. Far from it! The noise and bustle are deafening! Don't forget you are visiting the metropolis of the Empire, which has more than one million inhabitants.

To give you a little idea of what Rome has to offer, remember that there are as many as 37 gates into the city, 29 main roads, vast squares, hundreds of secondary roads, 8 bridges over the Tiber River, 856 private baths, 11 spas and 1,152 fountains,

190 granaries, 2 huge *macella* or meat, fish, and vegetable markets, 254 windmills, 11 forums, 10 basilicas, 36 triumphal arches, 2 circuses, 2 amphitheaters, 3 theaters, and even 28 public libraries! There are a good number of public urinals, too. These are appreciated by everyone but especially by the lively boys and young people chasing and joking with each other or just having a stroll or chatting with their friends under the arcades. The city grew up on the left bank of the Tiber River around the seven famous Roman hills called the Aventine, Palatine, Capitoline, Quirinal, Viminal, Esquiline, and Caelian hills, seven and a half centuries before the Emperor Augustus. The city developed over time and now has a 20 kilometer perimeter. This vast area is divided into 14 administrative districts called "regions" by order of the Emperor Augustus. Each of these districts is subdivided into quarters.

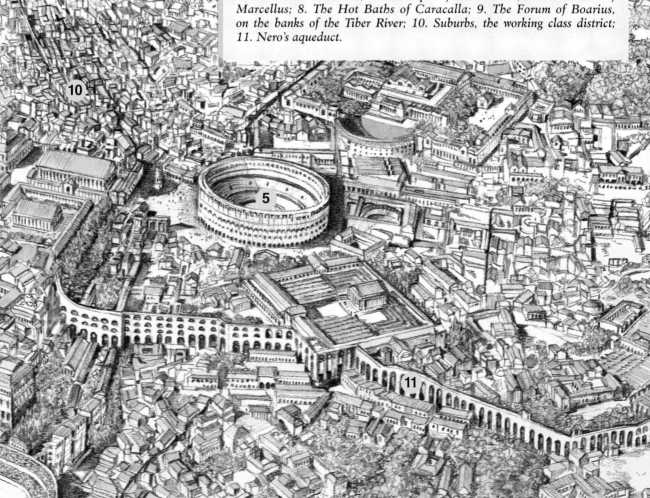

An aerial view of Rome

Here is a panoramic view of the capital of the Empire. A compact nucleus of houses stretches across the territory once only dotted with shepherds' huts. Splendid marble-covered buildings stand beside much simpler dwellings. There are plenty of green spaces too, where you can cool off on the hottest days.
The numbers on the illustration refer to the most important monuments and follow the order of description in your guidebook.
1. The Roman Forum; 2. The Curia, seat of the Roman Senate; 3. The Trajan Forum and the Trajan Column; 4. The Pantheon; 5. The Colosseum; 6. The Circus Maximus, on the slopes of the Palatine; 7. The Theater of Marcellus; 8. The Hot Baths of Caracalla; 9. The Forum of Boarius, on the banks of the Tiber River; 10. Suburbs, the working class district; 11. Nero's aqueduct.

Useful Information

As you enter the city, first climb up to the Capitoline Hill to pay homage to Jupiter the most venerated of the Roman gods. There you will find the Temple of Jupiter, the Capitolium. Then you can walk down to the Forum, go to the market along the banks of

the Tiber River or even walk through the Suburbs, the working-class district. The Suburbs is a poor, overcrowded quarter. It is full of stores! Barber shops, fabric stores, shoe repair, and foodshops, all offer the cheapest prices.

However, you need to take care! You had better go in the company of a centurion, it is not the safest of places! If you would rather buy from the most elegant shops in the city, go to the Field of Mars. This is a vast, level area, popular for taking open-air walks and for sporting activities. You should know that the well-to-do live for the most part in the hills, in luxurious villas or houses surrounded by trees and gardens.

To meet the famous celebrities in Rome, you have to go where they take their exercise, for example around the Temple of Diana up the Aventine Hill. On the Palatine Hill you can find the imperial palaces that dominate the *Urbs*, another Latin word for the capital, Rome.

A word of advice—try to avoid going out at night! You never know whom you might meet, and there are plenty of evil people around. Not to mention the risk of being hit by flying trash! Romans throw their trash out of their windows! Rome is dark at night, apart from the occasional torch. Anyway, if you need help, one branch of the police keeps the public order.

ROMAN MONEY

The same Roman money is used all over the Empire. This helps give uniform values to goods and possessions. It is essential for the efficient management of trade and commerce.

The most important coin is the gold aureus, the equivalent of 25 denarii, silver denarius coins. The denarius is worth 4 brass sesterces and 16 bronze as coins. Two as coins make a dupondius, and a quarter as makes a quadrans. A loaf of bread costs one as. A meal costs around two denarii. A soldier earns about 300 denarii per month.

To belong to the equestrian order, the most well-to-do social class in Rome, you need capital of around 400,000 sesterces. But this is nothing compared to the fortunes amounting to tens of millions of sesterces belonging to the richest men in the world, the Roman senators!

WHERE TO FIND FOOD AND LODGING

It will not be easy for you to find a hotel. The Romans would never dream of facing the difficulties and dangers of a long trip to go on vacation, or to visit other places.

Most upper-class travelers usually stay in the houses of friends or acquaintances where they are introduced by letters vouching for their good reputation and status.

The poorer classes and the merchants stay in taverns and hostels found along the main roads leading to the capital. Some of these offer simple food, such as fruit and wine produced locally. But be wary of the hotel owners! They have a reputation for being scoundrels and cheats!

If you enjoy a good meal, you can find food in the inns, but they enjoy the worst reputation of all! Food prepared days ago is on display in the open air! Enjoy!! At least the bill will not be too expensive.

ADDRESSES

How can you find someone's exact address in Rome? How can you plan where to meet? There are no street names, the houses are not numbered, and there are no nameplates on the doors. People use other forms of identification, such as a popular place, a famous statue, a column, a temple, a public building, or even a tree!

Only a few streets are really well-known because of a particular feature, like Shepherds' Street, where herds of sheep are always passing through. So people will talk vaguely about "at the entrance to...," "along the first stretch of...," or "at the top of the hill."

You will need to be patient when asking for help to find a person or a place.

DRESS

If you want to use the official Roman dress, you should wear a toga. This is a large piece of heavy, white, woolen cloth. It is not very practical so people prefer to change into the more comfortable tunic whenever possible. This is a really simple garment, just two pieces of material stitched together at the shoulders with two side seams and worn with a belt.

Tunics are worn by women too, but when they are in public, women must wear a stole over the tunic. The stole is the accepted dress code for the Roman matrons. It is a cloak that covers their figure almost entirely.

At home the Romans wear slippers. Leather sandals are worn outside. On special occasions or for ceremonies they wear closed leather boots. You have come to visit Rome, so you can avoid the official dress and wear what most travelers do, a simple, knee-length tunic and a cloak with a hood to protect you from the rain.

If it is hot you should wear a wide-brimmed hat. Make sure your bag where you keep your valuables is safely fixed to your belt. The mule you are riding will carry your luggage.

WHAT TO DO IN THE CASE OF ILLNESS

If you get sick during your visit to Rome, things could become complicated. Medicine is an experimental art for the Romans, based on the use of herbs and a few other natural remedies like leaves, roots, medicinal plants, animal fat, bizarre mixtures, and infusions. All the above are prescribed for and taken by the patients in the total absence of any official control by the public authorities.

The first real doctors came to Rome from Greece. They are extremely successful thanks to their rich clients. Go to them if you can afford it. These doctors even make house calls. If you prefer, they can examine you at a *medicinae*, a place rather like a doctor's office or at a kind of emergency clinic.

However, each wealthy family has its own private doctor. These are usually slaves who have followed a long apprenticeship. They will treat you according to your symptoms or misfortune. They will prescribe treatments, such as special diets, rest, or exercise.

One of the most frequently used remedies is a juice made from the roots of the silfius, a plant blessed with the most amazing curative qualities. It helps digestion, blood circulation, exhaustion, and convalescence. It can be applied to wounds and sores. It can be used as a poultice to treat abscesses and to eradicate corns. It is an antidote for the poisonous bites of snakes and scorpions. It cures sore throats, asthma, dropsy, swelling, jaundice, and pleurisy. It seems to cure almost anything except a toothache or grumpiness!

WHAT CAN YOU EAT IN ROME?

Bread is the basic element of a Roman meal. It is made from various types of flour. Brown bread is eaten by the poorer classes, the upper classes eat white bread, which is more refined and more expensive. Vegetables, such as lettuce, cabbages, leeks; legumes, like pulses, chickpeas, and broad beans; goat's cheese and olives are all plentiful. Ox meat, pork, wild deer, and donkey meat are popular. So is game, but fish is the most appreciated.

The mixture of sweet and savory flavors is typical of the Roman cuisine. Mint and vinegar, honey and cooked must (new wine or unfermented grape juice) with fruit puree, may be mixed in the same dish. Delicious!

Fruit and nuts are always served at the table. Romans also enjoy apples, pears, cherries, plums, grapes, walnuts, almonds, and chestnuts. Mushrooms are particularly popular.

The Romans eat three meals a day. They have a light breakfast with bread and wine or sometimes with cheese, eggs, fruit, and honey. At midday they eat a light lunch of eggs, fruit, and greens. Evening dinner is the main meal of the day and may begin mid-afternoon and last until far into the night. After a series of rich appetizers, numerous courses are served. The food is washed down with a drink made from a mixture of wine and honey. The richest tables are those prepared for the aristocrats. There you will find foods from all over the world together with vintage wines.

WHERE CAN YOU SHOP?

Rome is full of shops. The capital of the Roman Empire has no reason to feel inferior to the great cities of the Orient with their bazaars crammed with goods and their merchants always ready to haggle over prices.

Rome's business center is chaotic and noisy any time of day. Crowds of busy people teem through its streets. They stream into the stores, dawdle along the narrow alleys, and wander through the markets among the peddlers' stalls. There are auctioneers and traveling salesmen of all kinds. You can even find stalls selling secondhand books. There are merchants selling carpets and mats, and apprentice pork-butchers selling sausages, olives, and savory chickpea pies.

Family handicraft businesses selling the same kinds of goods, are all along the same street. For example, there is the street of the perfume makers, and the glass-makers' street.

To advertise, the shopkeepers use special signs. Some write on the walls, some have small sculptures or paintings with the symbol of their craft. Others use images of the god Mercury, the protector of merchants.

WEIGHTS AND MEASURES

The Romans employ various systems of measurement. The unit of weight is the *libra*, which comes from the Latin word for weighing scales. It is the equivalent of 327 grams and is divided into 12 ounces of 27 grams.

The *culleus* is the unit of liquid measure, equal to the contents of 20 jars (524 liters). In turn a jar holds about 26 liters.

The unit of measurement for wheat, flour, and most cereals in general is the same as one-third of a jar, that is 8.7 liters.

Surfaces are measured in *iugera*, equal to 2500 square meters, an area of about 35 x 70 meters, or the area of land a pair of oxen can plow in one day. The most frequently used measure of distance is the *miglio,* or mile (*mille passuum*). This is equal to one and a half kilometers. Then comes the *passus,* equal to 1,478 meters; the *pes* or *piede* (foot), about 30 centimeters long; the *gradus,* equal to two and a half feet.

Along the roadsides at every mile, you will find a stone, or a column, showing the distance in miles from that place to the nearest town.

MEASURING TIME: HOURS AND CALENDARS

The Romans are not very precise in the way they measure time. In the countryside time is calculated according to the agricultural work, which varies according to the season. The day's work depends more on the conditions of the light rather than a strict schedule. However, the Romans use hourglasses or sundials to calculate the passage of time.

The Roman calendar was reformed by Julius Caesar in 46 B.C. The length of a year was fixed as 365 days and 6 hours and divided into 12 months. Each month was divided into *kalendae*, (the first day of the month), *nonae*, (falling on the 6th or 7th day, depending on the month, and *idi*, (halfway through the month, the 13th or 15th). The ides of March would be March 15th, the calends of May, the 1st of May, and the nones of January would be January 5th.

So if you need to talk about when something happened, for the Romans each date will refer to the next calends, ides or nones. For example, if someone says, "two days before the ides of March," they mean March 13th.

CHILDREN IN ROME

As you walk through the narrow streets or through the squares in Rome, you will come across groups of children playing soldiers, judges, or galloping around pretending to be horses.

You might see them running after a kite, on a swing, or playing a game called the pot. This is a game where the child who is "the pot" sits on the ground and tries to throw a pebble to hit anyone within range. A top and a hoop are popular toys. A favorite game is to tie a few mice to a miniature cart and watch them charge forward in a panic, like a four-horse chariot in the arena.

In Rome only the rich send their children to school. Education is neither required nor free. Elementary school begins when children are between 6 and 7 years old. Lessons begin at dawn and finish in the early afternoon. Only very few privileged pupils continue their studies with a *grammaticus* or master after the elementary school. He introduces them to the works of Homer, Virgil, and Horace.

THE ROMANS, WHAT A CURIOUS PEOPLE!

Not all Romans are the same. As you walk through the streets, you are struck by the huge differences between the rich and the poor. The rich live in elaborate houses in the most elegant parts of the city while the poor, over half the population, live in the most degrading, poverty stricken areas. They live in dirty, overcrowded, small, dark rooms. They have hardly any belongings and often have to depend on public charity and gifts of food to survive.

Here comes an aristocrat followed by a procession of fawning *clientes*. He is wearing a toga of rich material and is reclining on a litter carried by his slaves. The crowd parts to let the noble patrician and the petitioners through. The patrician is wearing gold rings and a mocking smile. But who are those people who are panting under the weight of the litter? They are slaves in the service of his family and the private property of the head of the family. They do any kind of work, but especially the most exhausting or humiliating.

In Rome the slaves make up a third of the population, but there are also free citizens, who enjoy civil rights and take part in political decisions. All sorts of people from every part of the Empire live in the city plus, of course, the women. The women's job is to bring up the children and look after the house. They have no rights to take any part in public life.

The emperor is at the top of the social pyramid. He is the supreme head of the Empire and often makes on the spot decisions depending on his mood. Sometimes he is manipulated by one of his meddling councillors. He is a leader who is never questioned, not always loved, but one who affects the lives of everyone for good or evil.

The Roman Forum

You just have to start your visit to Rome in the Roman Forum, the huge square at the heart of the city. It lies among the Palatine, Capitoline, and Esquiline hills. It was paved many centuries ago at the time of the Etruscan kings, the Tarquins. Over time important public works and the completion of the drainage and sewage systems, especially the Cloaca Maxima, have allowed the marshy ground to be reclaimed.

The Forum is the Roman citizens' favorite meeting place. Quite early in the morning the crowds begin to gather here. Merchants come to do business. Money changers, moneylenders, busybodies, and lawyers, among others, trade, deal, and plot, seeking favors, clients, and money.

After the lunch break at around 2 P.M., when the administrative offices close, the square fills up with people. The ordinary people, including the idlers of the population, meet in the Forum to keep up with the news and to hear the latest gossip.

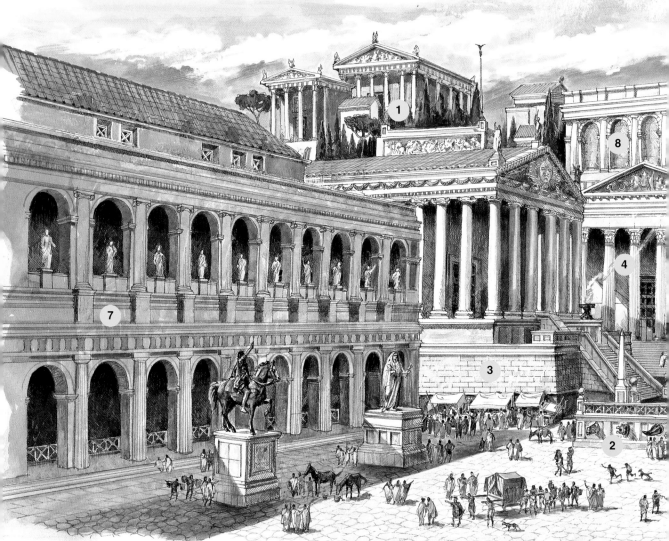

HERE THEY USED TO BURY THE DEAD!
Centuries ago, long before the Forum was built, this area was used as a burial ground. The first inhabitants of the Palatine and the Capitoline buried their dead here after the rite of cremation. At that time the dead body was burned on a pyre, and the ashes were kept in an urn. When the area became more populated, this practice ceased spontaneously since the Romans no longer buried their dead inside the city.

The funerals of the famous are celebrated here. Also the most influential public figures, always surrounded by a crowd of adoring followers, test their popularity, enhance their reputation, and increase their influence in the forum.

In the past, all the major events in the city took place in the buildings surrounding the Forum. Laws were made and trials and elections took place. The Forum was the center of all the most important religious and civic ceremonies. On special holidays, games were once organized in the square, but today these can take place in the amphitheater, the circus, or the stadium. Various grocery stores or craft stores called *tabernae* used to flourish around the edge of the square, but you can no longer find them.

Many of the public functions that used to take place here have been transferred elsewhere. Today the Forum is dedicated to the pomp of imperial power. It is the destination of the triumphal processions that climb up from the ancient sacred route, or *Via Sacra*, to the Temple of Jupiter on the Capitoline Hill.

Key to the illustration of the Forum.

The western side of the Forum, at the foot of the Temple of Jupiter on the Capitoline Hill (1), is one of the quarters of Rome most steeped in history and tradition. Here you can find the Comitium, seat of the oldest people's assembly and nearby is the Curia, the seat of the Senate. The Rostra, or speakers' tribune (2) is decorated with the figureheads of ships captured in battle. The Temple of Saturn (3). The Temple of Vespasian (4). The Temple of Concord (Harmony) (5). The impressive Septimius Severus Arch (6). The basilica of Julia and the basilica of Aemilia (7), used for business meetings and for the administration of the judicial system. The whole sector is dominated by the Tabularium (8), seat of the state archives. At the orders of Julius Caesar and later under other great Roman emperors extra Forums were built in the adjacent areas. So you will be able to see Forums dedicated to Caesar, Augustus, Vespasian, Nerva, and Trajan.

The Senate

You can visit the Curia, which stands at the northern end of the Roman Forum. This is the building that houses the Senate, the most important assembly in the state of Rome. The Senate has always been the most important institution in the empire. It holds responsibility for the entire political life of both the city and the empire. All the major economic, social, and military decisions are made here. Originally it was made up of the eldest members of the noble Roman families, the patricians. When Rome became a republic, the Senate increased from 300 to 800 members. At this time it began admitting members from the common people and from the Italian aristocracy who had previously been excluded from taking political office. Just imagine, to become a senator you had to possess at least a million sesterces! What is more, this wealth had to have come from agriculture, the chief economic activity of the Romans. Those who had become rich through business or in any other way were not allowed. This rule helps us understand just how conservative the Roman aristocrats were. They jealously guarded their power and privileges and were ready to oppose anyone who challenged their political role as leaders.

The Senate enjoys enormous prestige. The *senatus consulta*, decrees of the Senate, form the basis for the official publication of every law. They influence the magistrates, dictate the declarations of war, affect diplomatic negotiations, and award conquered territories. During the period of the Roman Empire, the Senate falls under the rule of the prince. The emperor names his senators personally, thus obtaining their almost total obedience.

Stormy sessions

At this time, the Senate meets twice a month, on the first and fifteenth, the calends and the ides. The senators enter the Curia at sunrise and stay until the evening. At times they pay homage to the emperor with gifts, (like the shield above), or write eulogies in his praise. However, they often shout, come to blows, and spend hours in irrelevant discussion.

A magnificent hall

The Curia Julia was begun by Julius Caesar
to replace the old Curia Hostilia. It was
inaugurated by Augustus. The Senate holds
its sessions inside a great hall 21 meters
high, 18 meters wide, and 27 meters long.
The senators sit along the longest sides.
The president of the Senate sits in the
middle at one end between two braziers.
Above him you can see a statue
of Victory which comes
from Taranto.

HOW DOES A SENATOR DRESS?

All Roman senators wear the official Roman dress,
the toga, but their togas have a special purple border.
They wear red leather boots. They also wear a costly
gold ring on their finger. This is a symbol of their
authority.

15

The Triumphal Procession

Why all this yelling and shouting? What's all this noise about? There are throngs of people crowding along the Via Sacra, or Sacred Way, to watch a triumphal procession. This is a combination of a military parade and a religious ceremony to celebrate the victory of the emperor and his army in war. After having spilt the blood of the enemy, it is traditional for the citizen soldiers to purify themselves with a ritual march around the most ancient city walls then pass under a triumphal arch.

The procession begins in the Circus Flaminius, crosses the Field of Mars, then goes through the Triumphal Gate, to the Forum of Boarius. From there it continues toward the Circus Maximus and finally reaches the Roman Forum through the Via Sacra.

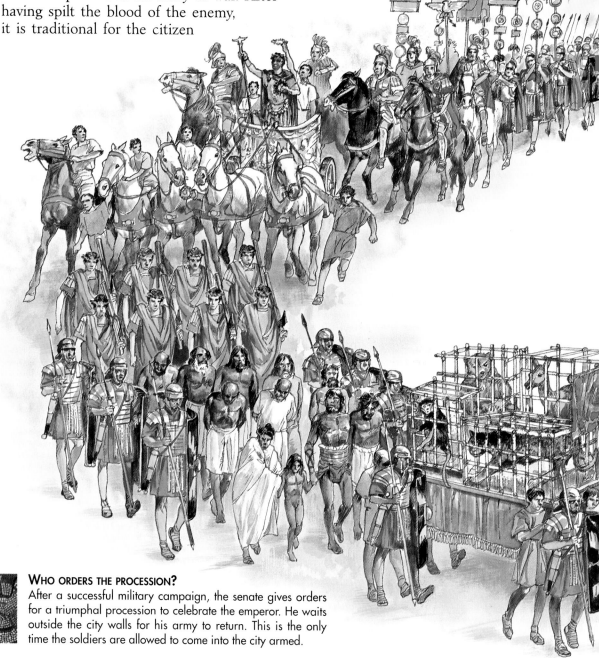

WHO ORDERS THE PROCESSION?
After a successful military campaign, the senate gives orders for a triumphal procession to celebrate the emperor. He waits outside the city walls for his army to return. This is the only time the soldiers are allowed to come into the city armed.

A Serious and Mocking Ritual

The emperor heads the procession. The army marches behind led by the officers on horseback. They are followed by the legionnaires singing songs either praising or mocking their commander. The crowd approves as the legionnaires incite the onlookers to shout, "I have triumphed!"

After crossing the Roman Forum, the procession climbs up the Capitoline Hill to stop in front of the Temple of Jupiter. The procession glorifies the general. He parades, together with his sons, in a chariot drawn by white horses. He wears a crown of laurel leaves and carries an ivory scepter, symbol of his command. His face is painted red, exactly like the face of the god Jupiter, to whom the temple on the Capitoline is dedicated. The temple is the final destination of the procession. After a sacrifice, all worship the emperor. He is considered a god.

The senators parade at the head of the procession with the trumpeters. Behind them are Roman citizens carrying the *titula*, or written notices bearing details of the victory being celebrated. They are followed by the spoils of war and the treasure captured from the enemy. This includes precious objects and perhaps rare animals, which draw wonder and amazement from the crowds.

The leaders of the defeated army are made to walk just in front of the victorious leader, together with the members of their families. Behind them come the prisoners, in chains. These long-haired, half-clad warriors speak an unfamiliar language. What a terrible spectacle!

The Sacrifice

Sacrifice is one of the most important religious practices used by the Romans. It is an act of atonement, asking for the mercy of the gods.

The Romans believe in many gods. This is a result of ancient beliefs in the forces of nature, a certain inheritance from the ancient Greek culture plus the influence of old myths and legends. Iuppiter, or Jupiter, is the most venerated. He is believed to be lord of the heavens, of thunder and lightning, "father of the gods," and protector of the state. Then comes Mars, the god of war; Iuno, or Juno, patron of women and of the family; Minerva, the warrior goddess of wisdom, arts, and sciences; Saturnus, or Saturn, god of the sowing season and agriculture; Vesta, protectress of fire and of the home; and Venus, the goddess of beauty and love.

The sacrificial rite follows special rules. Gifts in kind are made to the gods on fixed days, like part of the crops, the grape harvest, or dairy products. Animals are taken to the altar to be sacrificed. A sow, a sheep, and an ox are often sacrificed together. The solemn procession moves toward the *ara*, or sacrificial altar, which is always placed outside the temple. This is because the Romans believe the temple is the house of the god, a sacred place that the faithful must not violate. The priest waits for the victims, his head covered with the border of his toga. The victims are led by assistants at the sacrifice who, in turn, are guided by the youths from wealthy families who have been initiated into the rules of the sacrificial ceremony.

What is a *lustrum*?

The *lustrum* is the ritual sacrifice performed every five years at the close of the census on behalf of the Roman people. The censors, who are the civil servants responsible for the collection of tributes, or taxes, offer this sacrifice. An ox, sheep, and sow are sacrificed.

A Precise Ritual

The sacrificial rite is performed according to strict rules. All those taking part must undergo a ritual of purification. Then the procession advances in silence led by the sacrificer whose head is covered with a cloak. A flute player sounds the notes.

When the priest recites the special prayers, the one who performs the ceremony repeats the priest's words in a low voice, touching the altar with his right hand and touching his mouth with his left hand at the same time. A mixture of salt and a special kind of wheat flour is sprinkled on the heads of the animals to be sacrificed before their throats are cut by the attendant with the ax or by the one who uses a sharp knife.

Examining the internal organs

The Romans inherited an ancient method of predicting the future from the Etruscans. Some people are said to possess the gift of being able to "read" the internal organs, for example the liver, of the sacrificed animals to predict the future or understand the will of the gods.

The Romans consult the soothsayers, those believed to possess this gift, before making any major decision. The outcome of events is often influenced by a firm belief in this superstition. Bronze models of the liver, like the one on the left, were used as votive offerings or to teach trainees the art of divination.

The Trajan Column

While walking through the city center, you cannot miss the Trajan Forum. Before Trajan, other emperors gave the city famous squares dedicated to their name, but none created anything quite as splendid as this unique work. It is 300 meters long and 185 wide. An entire hill between the Quirinal and Capitoline hills was flattened out in order to build it.

The Forum looks like a square closed on either side by two enormous semicircular buildings, each surrounded by a portico. The one next to the Quirinal is extremely dramatic with its five stories used as a market. In the background rises the Ulpia Basilica, a huge building with five aisles. Beyond this you can see the temple dedicated to the Emperor Trajan after his deification.

Now you can see the Trajan Column. It is one of the masterpieces of Roman art! It measures 3.70 meters in diameter and is almost 30 meters high. It is completely covered with a marble frieze that spirals upward around the column. The decorations on this spiral frieze tell the story of Trajan's victorious military campaign against the people of Dacia who threatened his empire's northeastern borders.

You will discover a long tale told in realistic detail and decorated in vibrant color. Here are battles, camps, fortifications, and sieges. The building of this marvel was financed by the gold Trajan took from the Dacians!

WHAT IS INSIDE THE TRAJAN COLUMN?

Trajan's ashes were placed at the base of the column, so this monument is his tomb. Inside, a spiral staircase lit by slit windows, or embrazures, winds up to the top which is crowned by a bronze statue of the Emperor Trajan.

The Pantheon

You will find the Pantheon in the center of the Field of Mars, where the most powerful army in the world gathers to exercise. It is a temple dedicated to all the gods as well as to the deified emperor, raised in his turn to rank as an immortal.

Before the Pantheon was built, there was already a temple on this spot where the gods who protected the family of the Emperor Augustus were worshiped. The large square around the site is completely surrounded by beautiful porticos. If you look carefully at the Pantheon, you will realize what an exceptional construction it is. You enter through a magnificent portico supported by 18 pink and grey columns made of Egyptian granite. These are the tallest columns you can see in the entire city. From here you pass into an enormous, circular room, a rotunda, which supports a dome measuring more than 140 feet in diameter. The total height of the building is 140 feet, too. Once inside, you have the impression of being at the center of a gigantic sphere. The architects designed the

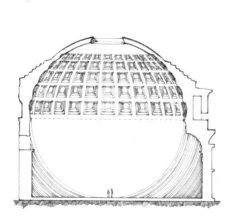

The biggest in the world!

The dome of the Pantheon is supported by a strong, cylindrical brick wall, 19 feet wide. It was created by pouring cement all at once into a gigantic wooden framework. On the inside the dome is decorated with recessed ceiling panels. This was made using light but resistant materials, such as pumice stone and tufa mixed with cement. Just think, you are looking at the biggest dome ever made. It weighs 5,000 tons!

Pantheon to symbolize the universe. Around the edge of the circular hall, you can find recesses in the wall containing statues of the gods. A brilliant beam of light shines from the *oculus*, or circular opening, in the center of the dome, illuminating the fabulous mosaic floor below. What a dramatic atmosphere! The Romans really knew how to build!

WHO BUILT THE PANTHEON ?

An inscription on the face of the Pantheon reads: "M(arcus) Agrippa L(uci) f(ilius) co(n)s(ul) tertium fecit" and honors those who built the first temple here. The Emperor Hadrian ordered the rebuilding of the temple, but the architect is not known. He remains as anonymous as the many workmen who were involved in completing this masterpiece of Roman architecture.

The Colosseum

If you visit the Colosseum you will be able to witness the awesome spectacle of the Roman games. These events take place at the same time as the main religious and civil festivals. You can hear a deafening roar. It is the sound of the crowd greeting the parade of gladiators as they make their triumphal entrance into the crowded arena, preceded by the magistrates, slaves, arms, and trophies. They are all accompanied by blaring trumpets and drumrolls. Last night they drank, feasted, and wept over their sad fate, together with that of their wives and children. But now they parade in their splendid costumes and plumed headdresses almost as scornful as film stars. Hurry up! Go and buy a ticket! It gives you the right to sit in a numbered seat and admire the athletes as they go around the arena and pay homage to the emperor who is sitting on a special platform and to the generals and senators sitting in specially reserved stands.

Everything is ready for the games to start. The pairs of gladiators who will duel with each other are determined in a draw. The judges check that the arms are according to regulations, then after a few skirmishes the real combat begins. The fighting is fierce and bloody; no blows are spared. The crowd cries, "Strike," "Cut his throat," and "Burn him!" The gladiators are not allowed to give in or to ask for mercy, and by evening only two are left to fight for the prize money.

The emperor and the crowd decide the fate of the loser. If the majority of the spectators shout out *"Missus!"* his life will be spared. If they shout *"Iugula,"* "Cut his throat!" he has no chance. The emperor's thumbs up or down will pass sentence. The winner is crowned with laurel and acclaimed by the public. He walks around the arena to the ovations of the spectators waving palm branches in appreciation of his victory. They shower him with coins that he collects on a silver plate.

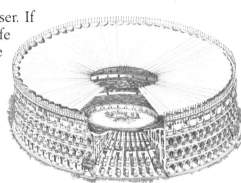

So many shows!

The Colosseum is the biggest amphitheater in the world and can hold 50,000 people. The central arena is surrounded by metal railings to protect the spectators from the fury of the wild animals. Famous battles are reenacted here. The arena can even be flooded to reenact famous naval battles. Famous sieges are reenacted, ending in real massacres. In the Colosseum you can watch capital punishments, and crucifixions and "enjoy" the terrible sight of men being eaten alive by wild beasts. On the hottest days, an enormous cloth stretches over the top of the building. It protects the spectators from the heat of the sun like an awning.

WHO ARE THE GLADIATORS?

They are slaves, prisoners of war, or criminals who have been sentenced to death, who are hired by special training schools or barracks in return for a grant of 2,000 sesterces. In the arena you can tell which training school they attended from their clothes, their arms, or their fighting styles. Some are armed with a large shield and a short sword. Others fight with a net and a trident, or three-pronged spear.

The Circus Maximus

If you are still looking for thrills after the shows in the Colosseum, you can check out the Circus Maximus. A huge, jubilant crowd of over 250,000 spectators greet the entrance of the parade led by the magistrate who will preside over the games. He is followed by the charioteers, the musicians, the priests, and statues of the gods. Before you enter, under the portico you can buy some refreshments to keep you going during the day.

As the crowd begins to roar their support, you can bet on one of the four teams in the race. Look, the four-horse chariots, their horses pawing the ground, are entering the starting gates along one of the shortest sides of the track. A white cloth is thrown from the tribune accompanied by a trumpet blast. These signal the start of the race.

The race ground is divided by a raised platform that runs down the center. It is 700 feet long. The competitors have to race seven laps, a distance of about 2 1/5 miles. On the platform there is an Egyptian obelisk, seven huge wooden eggs, and seven bronze dolphins that are lowered from time to time to show the number of laps the competitors have completed.

At the two ends of the central platform, we can see the winning posts. These are enormous stone cones around which the chariots have to turn a very sharp corner. This is the most exciting moment of the race, where the strength and agility of the horses and the courage of the charioteers are really tested. In a red-blue cloud of sand and mineral dust, the team that comes around the bend first, without turning over, wins the race and many big prizes.

The factions

There are four teams in the race. They can be recognized by their different colors: red , white, green, and blue. Each color represents a different stable. Every stable is managed by team masters, who are ready to pay huge fees to hire the best charioteers to race for them and be sure to win the support of the fans.

FROM SLAVES TO CHARIOTEERS

The charioteers are ex-slaves who have made their fortunes by winning the reckless chariot races. Both they and their legendary horses are famous throughout the Roman Empire. During the races they whip their horses enough to draw blood. They ride upright in the chariot, wearing a leather helmet and a tunic sporting the color of their team. They do not hesitate to stoop to tricks and cheating in order to win the big prizes.

A reflection of the universe

The architecture of the Circus Maximus aims to give a symbolic view of the world, the image of the Earth in the universe. The ditch that surrounds the central platform represents the sea. The pillar represents the sun. The twelve starting gates represent the twelve constellations in the zodiac. The seven laps around the race track stand for the orbit of the seven planets and the seven days of the week. Thus, the races themselves bring to mind the natural order of the universe, with the emperor at its head. At the races the spectators can receive coins, bread coupons, delicacies, free gifts, and even houses, farms, and plots of land as if granted by a god.

The Theater

What about spending a few hours at the theater? Hurry to find yourself a ticket! They are free and are taken very quickly! Find a comfortable seat, not too high up near the common people, or you will find it difficult to follow the action. The theatrical productions or *ludi scaenici* in Rome are supported by officials or rich citizens. Initially they were of a religious nature, but now they are for amusement only. They also provide an opportunity for the authorities to parade in public, including the emperor.

The audience is impressed above all by the scenery, the portrayal of the gods, the almost magical special effects, together with the dancing, singing, and music. The performances based on classical texts now play just a secondary role for the audience. Only the sudden appearance of a god or the prince brought into the action by clever technical devices captures their interest. It is traditional for the actors to wear special masks for productions of the works of the Roman authors Plautus or Terence. Masks were first

NO RESPECT FOR THE ACTORS!
The theatrical season in Rome lasts from April to November. All actors, even those performing with an established company, are thought to be practicing a degrading and socially unacceptable profession. Apart from the classical list of plays, many actors develop their skills as mimes, for comic or dramatic farce, or for pantomime, a special type of Roman theater in which all kinds of characters and plots are found.

used in classical Greek theater. In Roman tragedies, the public demand for gruesome scenes and cruel endings with real deaths increases. If their appetite is not satisfied on stage, they refuse to applaud and show their disapproval by whistles, catcalls, and insults.

The Theater of Marcellus

In Rome, the wooden theaters, which were constructed specially for each performance, are gradually being replaced by stone buildings. There are three theaters in the capital but the Theater of Marcellus is the largest. It can hold an audience of 14,000. The enormous semicircular sweep of steps measures 490 feet in diameter. It is supported on the outside by huge arches and ends on the inside in the orchestra, the last rows situated down nearest the stage. These places are reserved only for dignitaries. In front of the tiers of steps is the stage. It is 300 feet high and is decorated with recesses containing statues of members of the imperial family.

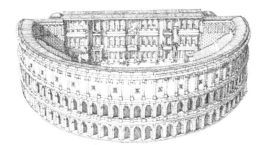

The Thermal Baths

During your stay in Rome, you will have realized that very few houses have toilets or bathrooms. This is why most people regularly go to the thermal baths. But they do not only go there to wash. For the Romans the thermal baths are somewhat like a recreation center. They go to meet their friends and to relax. They can do gymnastics or play games and talk with their friends in an extremely pleasant atmosphere. While some do weight-training or play ball games, others sit down for a beverage and a snack, gamble with dice or talk about current events.

The most famous thermal baths, or spas, in the city of Rome were built by the Emperor Caracalla. When you enter, the first place you go is the *apodyterium*, a kind of locker room. Then you go to the gym. After exercising to rid the body of sweat and dust, there is nothing better than a good sauna followed by a swim in the thermal pool. You pass through a succession of hot and cold rooms until you reach the hot steam room. From here you go into the pleasant, warm pool (1), then into the tepid, or lukewarm pool (2) that prepares you for the sudden temperature change that awaits you in the cold water pool (3). The last stage in the process is a visit to the *unctuaria*, a room like a beauty salon, where your body will be scraped and oiled to cleanse the skin of impurities. By now you will feel refreshed in body and mind, ready to end your day at the spa with a relaxing massage. Or perhaps you prefer a gentle walk under the arcades of the courtyard, in the open garden, among the sculptures and mosaics, or even in talking to friends, or glancing through a book in the reading room of the library. If you are really lucky, you might even catch a concert or hear a poet reading his works. Not bad, right?

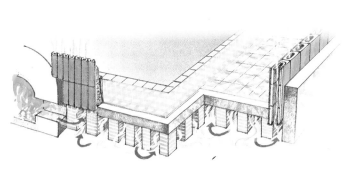

Central heating already existed!

A tried and tested central heating system allows heat to travel wherever it is required in the thermal baths. The furnace burns wood or coal. The hot air passes through cavities under floors built on piles of bricks. Then it goes through pipes placed in the hollow spaces between the walls, both in the rooms and in the swimming pool areas. In the sauna the temperature is so high that you have to wear wooden sandals to avoid burning your feet.

Opening times

The thermal baths open toward the end of the morning and close at sunset. More than 1,600 people a day use the spa. Entrance is free. A bell is rung as the public enters.

CAN MEN AND WOMEN BATHE TOGETHER?

No law prevents women from using the spa, bathing together with the men or taking part in the gymnastic exercises. However, many prefer to use the separate facilities reserved for women only.

The Cattle Market

Long before Rome became a great city there was flourishing trade and commerce along the banks of the Tiber near the Capitoline Hill. The Tiber River is an important route for transportation, and communication, and years ago work already began to strengthen its muddy banks. This reached its highest point in the construction of the Port Tiberino, the first commercial port of Rome. The goods coming from Greece, Egypt, the Orient, and the intermediate Phoenician ports arrive at the port of Ostia, on the coast. There they are transferred to smaller boats

From marshes to market

The legendary King Servius Tullius began the work to transform the area of the cattle market. He built a famous sanctuary dedicated to the goddesses of fortune and of the dawn, reclaimed the marshy plain and began the construction of a city sewer system with the completion of the Cloaca Maxima, *Great Sewer, which runs into the Tiber at Port Tiberino.*

Sacred and secular

Near the banks of the Tiber are two sacred buildings connected with commerce. The first is the temple of Portunus, dedicated to the god who is protector of the port. The second is the temple of Hercules Olivarius, patron of the oil merchants' guild. This temple was consecrated to Hercules by a rich Roman trader called Marcus Ottavius Erennius. He has made a fortune from the sale of olive oil used not only for cooking but also in the gymnasiums and in the making of cosmetics.

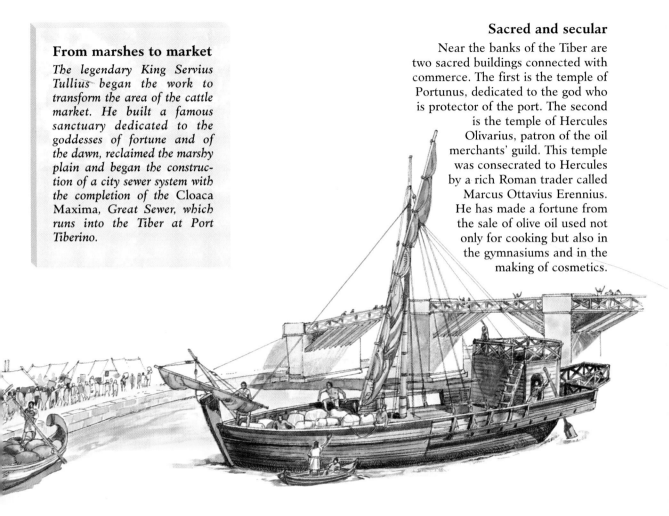

with sails or oars that carry them up river to Rome. The huge cargoes of wine, oil, wheat, spices, and salt, so precious for the preservation of foods, are unloaded, sorted, and stored in the *horrea,* or warehouses that have been built near the port.

The forum, or market, for fruit and vegetables is also in the same area. The market is an enormous, paved square, crowded with people. Nearby is the cattle market, particularly famous for its oxen. According to legend, Hercules grazed his herds here. Traditionally this area has always been the place to meet the many foreigners who come to Rome for all kinds of trade and commerce. They usually stay here while in Rome. There are merchants, money changers, commercial agents, diplomatic delegations, gamblers, foreigners, and tourists like yourself, who travel by sea.

WHAT STRANGE VESSELS!

If you watch the boats unloading at Port Tiberino, you are sure to spot an unusual kind of vessel. It is small, with a flat keel and looks like a barge. These boats are hauled along the banks of the Tiber River by oxen, buffalo, and sometimes even by slaves! They manage to come up river, even fully-loaded, without running aground in the shallow waters.

Wealthy Person's Home

The Romans are hospitable people, so you may well be invited to lunch at the home of a rich patrician or noble. His home, or *domus*, will be elegant and refined. The rooms will be spacious and well-lit. The walls will be decorated with expensive stucco-work and paintings. It will have beautiful mosaic floors and the decorations, furnishings, and sculptures will amaze you. This upper class house is almost always built on one level and from the outside appears plain and lacking in windows. The corridor leading from the street is crowded with clientes, people waiting patiently to be seen and granted favors or protection from the patrician. After a short wait here, you will be admitted. You will pass through the *fauces*, or corridor, into the atrium. This is a large, well-lit courtyard with an open roof. There is a pool in the center to collect rain water. In the atrium you will also find a small chapel dedicated to the gods believed to protect the home. The family safe is found here too, together with pictures of the family's ancestors.

In the more ancient types of homes, family life was centered around the atrium. Meals were taken and friends entertained here. In the more recent and more luxurious constructions, other rooms lead off from the atrium. These are bedrooms and two large rooms that are beside the real heart of the domus. In the past this room was reserved for the male head of the household, or *pater familias*. It was also used as the bridal bedroom. Today it is used to keep the archives and records of all the public works with which the family is connected.

Your host will receive you as he relaxes on the comfortable beds in the dining room. From here you can enjoy a view of a splendid garden surrounded by an arcade. In the center of the garden is a beautiful fountain or a fish pond with perfumed flowers and bronze and marble statues around the edge.

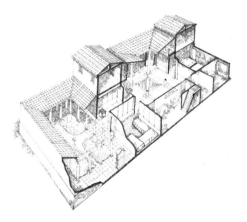

WHERE ARE THE FACILITIES?

The essential facilities are found in the more remote parts of the domus. Toilets and bathrooms are reserved for the family only. The kitchen is a small room with a brick fireplace, an oven, and a sink. The servants' rooms are dark and tiny. Outside the domus, on either side of the entrance, there are shops, or *tabernae,* which are rented to the shopkeepers by the patrician.

A building that serves as a status symbol

The domus is built to enhance the social position, culture, and wealth of its owner. Receiving the clientes is a public declaration of his power, influence, and prestige. His refined lifestyle is expressed through the ostentatious, or showy, practice of daily habits copied from the ancient Greeks, such as the custom of eating while lying down on the couch, strolling in the shade of the columns or showing the importance of the family's lineage in the documents stored in the atrium.

The Apartment Buildings

As you walk through the narrow streets of the suburbs, or working-class neighborhoods of Rome, you will realize how different are the lives of the majority of Roman citizens compared to those of the privileged nobles who live in a domus. Here the streets are crammed with busy crowds of people passing by, peddlers, loafers, deliverymen, slaves carrying sacks, thieves, dishonest people, all rushing around, in a mad dash, shouting at each other, everyone trying to make a living. The streets are lined with tabernae stores or shops. You can find craftsmen's workshops, food stores, and fruit and vegetable stalls.

The shops are at street level and above them are the working class apartments and lodgings. The scarceness of building land together with the constant growth of the population have encouraged the upward development of the housing projects in this area of Rome. The buildings are five or six stories high including the attics. They have been constructed as cheaply as possible, using poor materials and each one occupies a whole block or *insula*. They frequently collapse or catch fire! The walls are made of brick covered with wood or plaster and fitted with windows, balconies, and terraces.

The apartments are rented by their owners or leaseholders to families with a modest income. The higher up the building you go, the worse the living conditions become. The poorest people live on the top floors, crammed into wretched dwellings. There is no glass in the windows, so they are badly protected from the elements. Their only heating comes from braziers, and they have no running water or toilets, since the aqueduct supplies water to the ground floor only.

How are the working-class homes decorated?

The small apartments in the upper stories are very simply furnished. The tenants sleep on a low bed made of bricks covered with a straw mattress. There is a table and a few stools. A portable brazier is used for both heating and cooking. You have to carry your water from the nearest street fountain. Since you have no toilet, you have to use the nearest public toilets.

Fire! Fire!

Wooden beams, portable stoves, oil lamps, and burning torches used for lighting the apartments plus the limited water supply create a serious fire hazard in these buildings. But the huge number of dwellings destroyed by fire has allowed building speculation to grow very fast. Speculators have made their fortunes by buying the burned out ruins at extremely low prices only to rebuild in record time and resell for much higher prices.

HOW MUCH IS THE RENT?

The owners of the apartment blocks rent the upper stories for a five-year period to leaseholders who manage the upkeep and renting out of single apartments. The rent of even the most simple apartment is extremely high. It can cost 2,000 sesterces a month. (The average daily wage of a worker is five sesterces.)

The Appian Way

If you really want to get to know Rome, you should go outside the city walls and take one of the several consular roads that link the city with its territories. These roads are paved with slabs of basalt, an extremely hard stone, which makes them usable even in the worst weather. Along the way you will meet other travelers who come, like yourself, from the farthest regions of the empire. There will be farmers working in the fields, postal workers, families coming to pay homage to their dead.

If you leave the city by the Appian Gate, you can explore a stretch of the famous Appian Way. The landscape tends to bring an emotional response. In the shade of the pine and cypress trees, in the peace of the countryside, you will find a series of monumental mausoleums and family tombs where the remains of the families of the Roman aristocracy have been laid to rest. Just beyond the edge of the road, for several miles, you can stop and look at the more modest tombs. Many shrines are

The queen of roads

The Appian Way takes its name from the magistrate who built it, Appius Claudius Cieco. It is 4.10 meters wide and paved with huge blocks of basalt. There are sidewalks on either side made of stone and beaten earth. Every ten miles you will find a post station where you can stay overnight and change your horses. The Appian Way links Rome with Capua in the region of Campania. Then it turns inland towards Benevento and continues until it reaches the port of Brindisi on the Adriatic Sea. From there you can board a ship to Greece or the Orient.

decorated with the sculptured faces or figures of men and women from the middle classes. They were well-to-do tradesmen, civil servants or freemen. You can read the epigraphs, writings that speak about the lives of the dead, their achievements, and the cause of their death.

This whole area is the *necropolis*, the city of the dead. You will also come across small mounds or simple ditches made to hold the remains of the poorer people, mostly urns containing their ashes. Roman law forbids the burial of the dead within the city walls. Thus the dead are remembered by their picture or a statue, if their family can afford it. They seem to be standing at the roadside or to be looking from a window to greet those who pass by. This creates a very special atmosphere along the road and almost gives it a sense of eternity.

WHAT IS UNDER THE FLAGSTONES?
Quite special burial places are to be found in the subsoil. There are tunnels and cubicles hollowed out in the volcanic rock (the catacombs). Here the Romans bury the dead whom they do not cremate.

The Country Villa

All along the Appian Way, in the area surrounding Rome, you will not only find monuments to the dead but splendid villas belonging to rich landowners. These noblemen have chosen to move outside the city to supervise their estates more closely, for love of the peace the country life offers, or to take time out from the obligations required of their rank.

Their estates include both huge residences and impressive working farms. The wing reserved for the landowner follows the same layout as the aristocrat's home, or domus. There is an extra feature in the form of an open gallery, or loggia, around the edge of the building. From here the occupants can enjoy the view over the gardens, the estate, and the countryside, and be sheltered from the summer heat.

In the real country house live the farmer and his wife, together with the families of the free laborers and the slaves. Another building houses the facilities, which include the oil-mill for crushing the olives for olive oil, the wine cistern, the wine-presses, the store for agricultural tools, the jars for keeping olive oil and cereals, and the stables.

HOW DO THE SLAVES LIVE?
As a cheap work force, slaves provide the basis of the Roman economic system. They are bought and sold like any other goods and belong exclusively to their owner who can exercise every right over them, including that of life or death. They are exploited in the countryside, down the mines, and in the city. Sometimes they rise to positions of trust with the families they serve and do occasionally win their freedom.

The land, the vegetable garden, and the plantations are cultivated by a large number of slaves. They are supervised by the farmer who has to feed and dress them. As compared to the past, small farms are dying out in favor of large estates with a single landowner. These are called *latifundium*. Vines and olive trees are still grown, but there is a tendency to produce an ever-increasing harvest of wheat and other cereals.

Precious wines!

Agriculture is the most important economic activity in Rome. It has always been the traditional source of wealth for the landowning aristocracy. Wine is the most valued product. Italy enjoys a reputation for great wines throughout the Empire. The vines are cultivated with extreme care in the hilly country. They are planted in one meter-deep holes and tied to a tree, usually an elm, which guides the vines. One of the best wines is the Falernum, which is produced by the vine-growers of the northern Campania region, between the Savo River and the Volturno River.

The Port of Ostia

At the mouths of the Tiber River you will find the city of Ostia and Pozzuoli, the most important port in Roman Italy. Pozzuoli is the most natural outlet for the capital, which is only 20 miles away. The goods that arrive from many parts of the world go up the river to supply the city. Since the time of the Punic Wars, Ostia has performed the double function of port of call and naval base for the Roman fleet.

The city has more than 20,000 inhabitants and appears flourishing and hardworking. You will find squares, stores, commercial offices, trade associations, and elegant residences. The enormous volume of traffic encouraged by the rapid development of Rome has made it indispensable to build another port beside the original one constructed by the Emperor Claudius. The new port ordered by the Emperor Trajan has been joined to the huge, original basin protected by two piers, which jut out into the open sea, and which is connected to the Tiber River by an artificial canal. It was dug out of the dry land and is a hexagonal shape. Each side

GOODS FROM ALL OVER THE WORLD
Ten million sacks of wheat are unloaded and stored in the warehouses each year. The ships that moor alongside the wharfs bring all kinds of goods: spices and gems from Sri Lanka; wine and honey from Greece; parchment and horses from Asia Minor; iron and wood from Dalmatia; glass and leather from the Orient; wheat from Egypt; salt from Spain; and copper and tin from Britain.

measures over 1,170 feet. This second port includes a vast area of *horrea,* or warehouses, a lighthouse, thermal baths, a theater, a temple dedicated to Hercules, and a colossal statue of the emperor.

In the horrea, storage areas open onto a courtyard surrounded by an arcade. Carts cannot pass through the narrow entrance gates so the goods unloaded onto the piers have to be carried by manual workers like longshoremen. You can see them toiling along the wharfs under the weight of chests, sacks, and baskets.

Navigation at sea

Sailors sail the high seas without the help of navigational instruments. They calculate their position by observing the sun and the stars, and these voyages are limited to the periods of better weather between March and October. Coastal voyages, however, continue all year-round, and the sailors have to stop somewhere overnight. In the Roman world, transporting goods by sea is much cheaper than transporting them over land.

Roman ships can carry an impressive cargo!

The most common Roman transport vessel is a ship that is 80–100 feet long and 25–33 feet wide. It is quite a squat shape with a round keel. It has a square sail and its prow is decorated with a figurehead shaped like a swan's neck. The ship has an upper balcony deck for the steersman and can carry between 3 and 4 thousand jars (which corresponds to a cargo of between 110 and 180 tons).

The Aqueducts

One of the most extraordinary achievements of Roman engineering is the construction of the aqueducts, built to supply the city with water. At first, this project was financed with the money obtained during military campaigns, then later during the period of the Roman Empire, the State Treasury reserved the right to allot the necessary funds to these important public works.

Once the technical problems connected with the use of arches and vaults have been solved, the major obstacle to the success of such a project is to guarantee a continuous flow of water even when challenged with differences of level or hollows in the land. From its source the water flows in an underwater pipe that keeps a gentle but constant rate of descent, along the length of its journey.

To keep the gradient stable, the Roman engineers employ the cleverest forms of canalization that take advantage of a series of wells for aeration and maintenance. They do not hesitate to level the land where necessary, to build arcades or canal bridges of the most unusual dimensions which may connect entire valleys.

At the entrance to the city, the water is decanted in special tanks. Then it passes through a huge tank, where it is directed into the network of lead or terracotta pipes serving the city. From here it is distributed to the houses, the public baths, the swimming pools, gardens, and fountains.

WHO BUILDS THE AQUEDUCTS?
Above all, the slaves and bricklayers build the aqueducts and keep them working, looking after their maintenance. The engineers, who are almost always soldiers, are responsible for their design. Aqueducts are to be found all over the Roman Empire. They have become a model of civil architecture.

Running water for the capital

The oldest aqueduct was built by the censor Appius Claudius, which is why it is called Aqua Appia. It runs for more than 15 miles from the springs south of Aniene as far as the southeast quarters of the city. Another ten enormous aqueducts, each with several branches, have been constructed to supply the capital: the Anio Vetus (more than 37 miles long), the Aqua Marcia (the longest, over 56 miles long), the Aqua Tepula, the Aqua Julia and the Aqua Virgo, the Aqua Alsietina, the Aqua Claudia and the Anio Novus, the Aqua Traiana and to complete the list, the Aqua Alessandrina. The aqueducts supply water for the daily consumption of the inhabitants of Rome, providing more than a million cubic meters per day.

The Army

As you wander through the streets of Rome, you will soon realize that the emperor and his followers are always escorted by numerous soldiers. These are volunteers serving a short term of military service and very well paid. They are armed with fasces, (a bundle of rods bound up with an axe in the middle, its blade projecting), shields, and rods, the symbol of supreme authority. This is the Pretorian Guard, the personal guard of the ruler. It is made up of 9 groups, 3 of which are stationed in the capital, in the area called the Castra Praetoria, (*castra* is the Latin word for military camp). This garrison of 4,500 men is the only one present in the city. The troops operating outside the city walls are called the *legiones*. They are constantly engaged in defending the frontiers of the Empire, checking invasion attempts, putting down rebellions and conquering new territories. Do not forget that Rome created its Empire thanks above all to the army, a highly efficient military machine. The army is also an instrument of social control. Whoever enrolls in the army receives a regular salary. At the end of his military service, each soldier receives from the state a plot of land to cultivate, either in the provinces where he has served, or in one of the more recently conquered territories. When the soldiers leave the army, Roman citizenship is given to anyone who does not already possess it, including the foreign auxiliaries who have fought for the Empire.

mounted soldier

legionnaire

lance bearer

standard bearer

HOW IS A LEGIONNAIRE ARMED?

The legionnaire is protected by several types of armor. First he wears a breastplate covered with metal plates to protect the chest and the shoulders, and with leather strips above the legs. On his feet he wears special boots and on his head a helmet with protection for the neck and cheeks. He carries a rectangular shield made of leather reinforced with iron. He holds it to defend his body. A wide belt holds the sheath of a short sword. In his hand he carries a long lance.

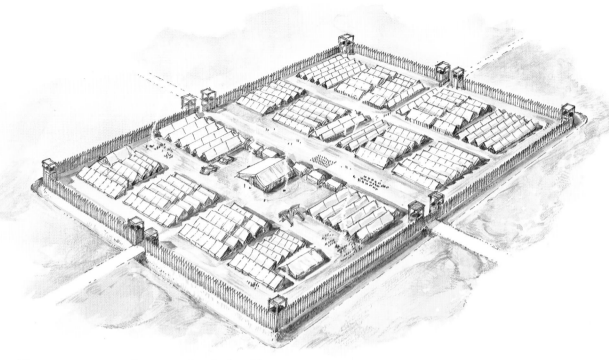

The army camp, almost a city in itself.

All along the frontiers of the Empire, the army is quartered in camps that follow the exact plan of a Roman city, but in miniature. It is quadrangular in shape and has all the necessary facilities, workshops, granaries, storehouses, a market, thermal baths, and a hospital. The camp is surrounded by a ditch, moat or rampart, by a stockade or even by a solid wall. Two main roads cross the camp, one from north to south, the other from east to west. At the point where they meet, in the middle of the camp, you can find the commanding officer's tent and the general headquarters, surrounded by the soldiers' quarters.

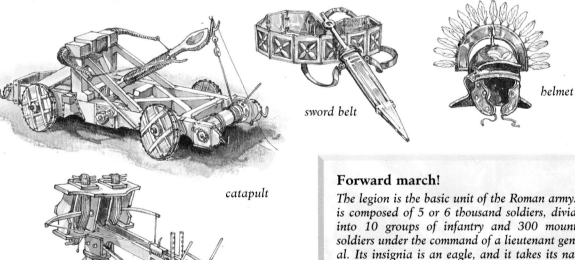

sword belt

helmet

catapult

Machine that hurls large stones

Forward march!

The legion is the basic unit of the Roman army. It is composed of 5 or 6 thousand soldiers, divided into 10 groups of infantry and 300 mounted soldiers under the command of a lieutenant general. Its insignia is an eagle, and it takes its name from its number (for example "the thirteenth"), the person who established it, ("Claudian"), or from a divinity, ("Martian," from the god Mars). In battle the legionnaires use a three-line formation. The lance bearers form the first line, armed with long lances. Then come the princes, armed with swords and shields. The veterans in reserve bring up the rear. Each of these lines forms a division of the legion, under the command of a centurion, who gives orders to a standard bearer who in turn transmits them to the troops.

Present-Day Rome

Present-day Rome is an exciting city of over three million people. It is one of the world's great cultural centers, the capital city of Italy, and the administrative and spiritual center of the Roman Catholic Church. This lovely city has all the problems of a modern city, such as traffic jams and pollution.

However, Rome's central core is still almost untouched by 20th century development. Many of the buildings and monuments of Imperial Rome remain, and many of the sites mentioned in this book can still be seen. There is much for tourists in Rome each year to visit and enjoy. Here we are going to describe some of the remaining splendors of this ancient city. You might plan on seeing these for yourself.

Colosseum

The Colosseum is probably the most famous landmark in Rome. It was built on the Esquiline Hill by the Flavian emperors. The biggest arena in the ancient world, it was completed in 82 A.D. Lightning, earthquakes, and vandalism have damaged it. In more recent years, it has suffered from traffic vibration and pollution. All the marble seats have disappeared. But it is still a truly spectacular sight and a "must" for tourists.

As you gaze at this huge amphitheater, colorful images of staged naval battles, battered gladiators, and ferocious wild beasts will surely come to mind. You may even imagine the roar of the bloodthirsty crowd.

A recent project has begun using the world-famous monument to draw international attention to the evils of capital punishment. This famous symbol of bloodshed and terror is to become a symbol of mercy. In December 1999, the arena was illuminated with golden lights. These lights will be turned on each time somewhere in the world a death sentence is changed or when a nation abolishes capital punishment completely.

Roman Forum

The ruins of the Roman Forum, center of the religious, political, and commercial life of Ancient Rome, stand in the middle of modern Rome. For a panoramic view of the Forum, climb up the Capitoline Hill to a terrace at the southeast corner. From here you will see the Forum's most important remains. With a guidebook in hand, you will be able to spot the Temple of Saturn, Septimius Severus' Arch, Vespasian's Temple, the Temple of the Vestals, and the Temple of Concord.

Baths of Caracalla

Take the Roman Metro Subway to the Circus Maximus station, and then walk to the Roman Baths of Caracalla. This gigantic group of ruins forms one of the most impressive images of Ancient Rome. It is said to have held 600 bathers at a time. Beautiful mosaics once decorated the baths, and splendid fountains and sculptures once stood here. You can still see some of these.

Besides the baths were several libraries, a gymnasium, and a stadium. Notice the floral designs and columns with figures of Roman gods. In the northwest corner of the grounds, you can visit part of the vast network of underground rooms under the baths. If you are lucky, you might get to hear one of the operas that are held at the baths every summer.

The Appian Way

Celebrated by poets as "the queen of long distance roads," the first few miles of the Appian Way are still flanked by striking monuments. The foundations of the six-meter-wide road were made of heavy stone blocks, cemented together, over which blocks of lava were expertly fitted to make a good traveling surface. As you will see, it has proved amazingly durable.

The city stretches of the road include the streets from the Baths of Caracalla to the Saint Sebastian Gate, after which the road is lined with ancient trees. Many stretches are still covered with lava blocks bordered with sidewalks.

Circus Maximus

The Circus Maximus was the largest of the Roman arenas and one of the largest sports arenas ever built. This "U"-shaped structure had seats on three sides and a low wall down the middle that chariots raced around. Rebuilt in the 1st century B.C. under Julius Caesar, the arena could seat about 150,000 spectators. Further enlarged by later emperors, it reached its greatest size under Constantine in the 4th century A.D. to seat 250,000. The seating capacity was greater than any later stadium. Today, nothing but the site, between the Palatine and Aventine hills remains.

Trajan's Column

Trajan's Column, a marble Doric monument erected between A.D. 106–114, survives almost intact today. It stands on a high cubic base where a chamber was to serve as Emperor Trajan's tomb. An entrance in the base leads to a large room that is said to have once held a golden urn with Trajan's ashes. The bronze statue of the emperor on top was replaced in 1587 by a statue of Saint Peter.

Forum Boarium

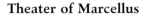

The area corresponding to the old Forum Boarium, or Cattle Market, is now called the Piazza della Bocca Verita, one of the most picturesque places in Rome. The square is surrounded by buildings erected using many materials taken from the ancient Roman structures. You can also see two exceptionally well-preserved Roman temples. One is a small temple called Temple of Fortuna Virilis, built around 100 B.C. Nearby you can see the temple of Hercules Olivarius, a round building with many columns. On the north side of the square stands the marble cube called the Arch of Janus.

Theater of Marcellus

This building was begun under Julius Caesar and finished in 13 A.D. by Augustus. Augustus dedicated it to his nephew Marcellus, who died very young. The complete foundation of the wedge-shaped sections of seats, still exists under the building, although nothing remains of the stage. However, all of the external arches and columns are well preserved.

Pantheon

The Pantheon was begun in 27 B.C. by the Emperor Agrippa as a temple and was completely rebuilt by the Emperor Hadrian between A.D. 118 and 128. This temple of all gods is remarkable in its size, construction, and design. It is a circular building of concrete faced with brick. Its great concrete dome rises from the walls, and a front porch of Corinthian columns holds a gabled roof with a triangular pediment. The huge 23-foot-high bronze double doors that you enter are the earliest known of their kind. The dome was the largest built until modern times, 140 feet in diameter and 72 feet above its base.

The main area, a huge circular space, is lit only by the light that streams in through the 26-foot oculus, or "eye," opening at the center of the dome. It is perhaps one of the first of several important buildings of antiquity designed to beautify the interior rather than the exterior. The outside is plain, but the interior is lined with colored marble.

In A.D. 609 the Pantheon was dedicated as the Church of Santa Maria Rotonda or of the Martyrs. Some small changes have been made. But, except for those, this building is in its original form. This best-preserved building of ancient Rome is very popular with tourists. Two Italian kings are buried here. So is Raphael, the great artist. You may see beautiful flowers that are still placed on his tomb by admirers.

Claudian Aqueduct

If you catch a train from Rome's Termini Station to visit the Frascati wine-growing region about 13.5 miles to the north, you will see the huge, yet picturesque ruined arches of the Claudian Aqueduct begun in A.D. 35 and completed by the emperor Claudius in A.D. 49. This water supply system was 40 miles long, with 8.5 miles on the surface. It carried the water from two springs Cerulea and Curzia—along the Via Sublacense into Rome. If you prefer to travel by car or bus, the road also passes close to these ruins.

Some Important Dates

The foundation of Rome • The small herdsmen's village developed on the Palatine hills, near the Tiber River, around 753 B.C. During the next century it grew into a town which united the tiny settlements scattered across the seven hills: Aventine, Palatine, Capitoline, Quirinal, Viminal, Esquiline, Caelian. The foundation of the city is associated with the legend of Romulus and Remus, the twin brothers who founded the settlement that became Rome.

The Monarchy • Rome became an important center thanks above all to the Etruscans who subdued and dominated it during the 6th century B.C. The city was governed by a king who was assisted by a Senate. The seven kings traditionally associated with the city in this period were Romulus, Numa Pompilius, Tullus Hostilius, Ancus Marcius, Tarquinius Priscus, Servius Tullius, and Tarquin the Proud.

The foundation of the Republic • After the Tarquins, the Etruscan kings, had been driven from the city in 510 B.C. the republican period began for Rome. The king was replaced by two magistrates, the consuls, who held the post for one year. The Forum was paved during this time and became the heart of city life. In 390 B.C. Rome had to defend itself from the invasion of the Gauls who sacked the city. From 390 B.C. until the Samnite Wars (343–290 B.C.) Rome consolidated its domination over Lazio and the surrounding regions. After the wars against Pyrrhus, the king of Epirus (280–275 B.C.), and the victory obtained at the end of the Punic Wars (264–146 B.C.) over its rivals from Carthage, Rome extended its domination of the Mediterranean by conquering Macedonia (168 B.C.) and Greece (146 B.C.).

During the 1st century B.C., Roman society went through a period of bloody civil wars. These began with Marius and Sulla (88 B.C.) and continued with Caesar and Pompey until the creation of the first triumvirate (Caesar, Pompey, and Crassus) in 60 B.C. This dealt a decisive blow to the democratic structure of the city for five centuries.

The Empire • In 27 B.C., Augustus Caesar's nephew, founded the principality, keeping the control of foreign affairs and the army for himself but leaving the administration of the state in the hands of the magistrates. Peace was maintained thanks to a policy of wise concessions to the Italic peoples who were subjugated as a consequence. They were all guaranteed Roman citizenship. By now Rome was a great power and expanded its domination over the whole of the Mediterranean and a large part of the Middle East.

Rome at the height of its glory • From 98–117 A.D., with Trajan at the head of the state, the Roman Empire reached the height of its influence and area. Trajan's successors, beginning with Hadrian, were concerned above all with reinforcing and consolidating this complex political, military and administrative structure against every threat that came from outside.

The Late Empire Period • The 3rd century A.D. saw the beginning of a difficult period in Roman history. This was due to political, religious and social reasons together with pressure from the populations living beyond the *limes*, who threatened the frontiers of the Empire.

New cults and religions were developing, including Christianity, which contrasted strongly with the imperial ideology from its beginnings.

In 395 A.D., the Emperor Theodosius divided the Empire into two parts: the Eastern Roman Empire, with Constantinople as its capital, and the Western Roman Empire.

In 476 the Ostrogoths invaded and sacked Rome, thus bringing the Western Roman Empire to its end. The last Roman Emperor to rule over the Western Roman Empire was the young Romulus Augustulus who reigned for one year only (475–476).

The most famous emperors
Augustus (27 B.C.–14 A.D.), Claudius (41–54), Vespasian (69–79), Titus (79–81), Nerva (96–98), Trajan (98–117), Hadrian (117–138), Caracalla (211–217), Aurelian (270–275).

Glossary

Note: Words are followed by respellings given in parentheses. Syllables that are stressed are in capital letters.

apodyterium (uh-POD-i-TARE-ee-um) the room near the entrance to the spa used as a locker room

ara (ARE-ah) the altar where sacrifices are carried out and where animals are sacrificed

castra a military camp

cisiarii (KIZ-ee-ARE-ee) special coaches used as taxis or a form of public transportation in Rome

clientes (KLEE-en-tase) people who request special favors from an important family, or who owe favors to them. They often receive economic or legal protection. In return they undertake never to take legal action against them and to ransom them from prison should the need arise.

edicta (ee-DICT-ah) announcements painted in red on the walls in the city advertising the gladiator fights

epigraph (EH-pi-GRAF) inscriptions on tombstones for the purpose of conserving or exalting the memory of the dead person

fauces (FAW-case) narrow corridor leading to the atrium, or entrance hall, of a Roman house

horrea (hor-EYE-ah) vast warehouses built in areas where there is a concentrated volume of goods to be stored, for example, near ports or markets

insula (IN-sul-uh) a block of multistoried public houses built between two parallel roads

latifundium (LAT-i-FUN-dee-um) a vast extension of land owned by one rich landowner

legiones (LEG-ee-OH-nase) a unit of the Roman army made up of infantry and mounted soldiers, numbering between 5 and 6 thousand men

limes (LIM-ase) fortified line along all the frontiers of the Roman Empire, the basis of the Roman system of defense

ludi scaenici (LUD-ee • SKY-ni-ki) theatrical performances with actors, elaborate scenery, and special effects

macella (mah-CELL-uh) city market for the sale of meat, fish, fruit, and vegetables

medicinae (MED-i-SIN-eye) something like a doctor's office or an emergency clinic

necropolis (neh-CROP-oh-lis) or "city of the dead," the area outside the city walls where the dead are buried according to the directions of the authorities

oculus (AH-cue-lus) wide opening at the center of a dome that allows light and air to enter

paterfamilias (PAH-tur-fa-MILL-ee-us) recognized head of the Roman family, who exercises his authority over all its members including the slaves

senatus consulta (sen-AH-tus • cun-SUL-tah) decrees passed by the Senate group that have the same value as laws

spina (SPEEN-ah) long platform built of stone and brick that divides the stadium in half lengthwise. The chariots race around this platform.

stationes (STA-shun-ace) post stations where you can stop, change horses, eat, and rest. These stations or stops are found at regular distances along the Roman roads

tabernae (tab-ERR-nigh) stores selling food or handicrafts

titula (TIT-you-lah) placards bearing inscriptions celebrating the achievements of victorious military leaders; they are carried at the head of the triumphal processions

unctuaria (UNCK-tu-ARE-ee-uh) a kind of beauty salon at the thermal baths where the body was carefully shaved and massaged with oils to free the skin from impurities

Urbs (ERBS) the other name for the capital city of Rome

Further Reading

Abbott, Frank F. *The Common People of Ancient Rome: Studies of Roman Life and Literature,* Biblo, 1965.

Babcock, John and Graham I. Tingay. *The Romans and Their Empire.* (History Matters series). Dufour, 1991.

Corbishley, Mike. *Everyday Life in Roman Times.* (Clues to the Past series). Watts, 1994.

Corbishley, Mike. *Rome and the Ancient World.* (Illustrated History of the World series). Facts on File, 1993.

Dowswell, Paul. *Roman Record.* (Newspaper Histories series). EDC Publishing, 1998.

Ganeri, Anita. *How Would You Survive As an Ancient Roman?* (How Would You Survive? series). Watts, 1995.

Hodge, Peter. *Roman House.* (Aspects of Roman Life series). Longman, 1971.

Honan, Linda and Ellen Kosmer. *Spend the Day in Ancient Rome: Projects and Activities That Bring the Past to Life.* Wiley, 1998.

Lamprey, Louise. *Children of Ancient Rome.* Biblio, 1967.

Nardo, Don. *Life in Ancient Rome.* (Way People Live series) Lucent, 1996.

Shuter, Jane. *The Ancient Romans.* (History Opens Windows series) Heinemann, 1998.

Snedden, Robert. *Technology in the Time of Ancient Rome.* Raintree Steck-Vaughn, 1998.

Index